Rave Rev Your Buttons

"*RESET Your Buttons* carries importance to the business owner and executive looking to get back to basics in today's economy, speaking to the human nature of the individual. Mary Elizabeth's writing style is also functional for everyone, regardless of their background in personal and group dynamics. <u>*Caveat*</u>: Much like Cliff Notes, if you don't hire *S.T.A.R. Resources*, you are missing the beauty of the literature!"

Bob Abeel, Regional Manager – Noteworthy

"I was anxious to go out and buy this book after reviewing the first few pages. I immediately wanted to send it to my children who are now in the adult world of relationships, both personal and in the work world and say 'see, it's OK not to know how to do everything perfectly; not to know what to expect; not to know exactly how to be ready; it's really OK NOT TO KNOW!!!' As Mary Elizabeth points out, we have never experienced the next moments of our lives before----so how can we possibly know how to live them??

Mary Elizabeth reminds us that our reactions to situations at home, at work and other social arenas are all based on our core values and how we respond to challenges to those values. The goal is to be a self-directed person, not an "other directed" person; the goal is to be someone who sets, or re-sets our own buttons - taking away the power of others to 'push our buttons.' We can learn to be a person who says 'I choose to' rather than a person who says 'I have to.'

This book is a 'how to' for all of us to learn how to be the kind of person we want to be and know we can be ... and have the tools to be. We just have to do some work to get there!"

Jay Polzien, VP of Marketing - Artwear Embroidery, Inc.

"I really liked reading *RESET Your Buttons...* it was as if Mary Elizabeth Murphy was having a personal conversation with me. It was a lot of fun! I jotted down some terrific ideas I picked up while reading it. Great job!"

Keith Ayers, President - Integro Leadership Institute

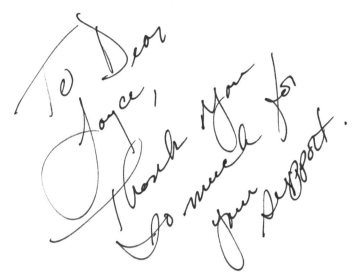

To Dear
Joyce,
Thank You
so much for
your support.

RESET Your Buttons
(and create relationships that work!)

Remember to
use your "RESET
MinDSET"

M ARY E LIZABETH M URPHY

authorHOUSE®

Love
Mary Elizabeth

AuthorHouse™
1663 Liberty Drive
Bloomington, IN 47403
www.authorhouse.com
Phone: 1-800-839-8640

First published by AuthorHouse 9/15/2009

ISBN: 978-1-4490-0449-1 (e)
ISBN: 978-1-4490-0624-2 (sc)

Library of Congress Control Number: 2009907574

Printed in the United States of America
Bloomington, Indiana

This book is printed on acid-free paper.

This book is dedicated to my parents John Patrick and Elsie Murphy, my husband Gary Erdakos, my brother Michael Patrick Murphy and my sister Kathleen Mary Gulch for all their love, commitment, support and willingness to learn alongside of me while I continue to "RESET my buttons."

ACKNOWLEDGMENTS

When it came time to write the acknowledgment for this book I began stressing (the-lie-awake-all-night-can't-eat kind) over it. Racing through my head was this thought, "How could I acknowledge everyone without leaving anyone out? Because, God forbid I should forget someone and hurt their feelings - thereby causing their or my buttons to be pushed!"

And then it hit me: who put all those wonderful people into my life? Every single soul that has touched my life came into my life thanks to God. So to God I give thanks, for all of you who have touched my life. You each have contributed to M.E. and therefore contributed to the creation of this book.

To God for sending you and to you for being you I give thanks.

Joyfully yours,
Mary Elizabeth

CONTENTS

Prologue xi

Chapter One: Recognition 1

Chapter Two: Expectations 15

Chapter Three: Sense of Self 31

Chapter Four: Emphasize Core Values 47

Chapter Five: Take Stock 63

Chapter Six: DISARM 75

Afterword 85

PROLOGUE

> One of the worst things we can do to ourselves and our self-esteem is to utter the words, "Somehow I should know."

Much of my youth was spent listening to my mother's sage advice and wisdom. She used to say things like "Why do you let them push your buttons? You need more self-esteem."

She would say it so often that it got to the point that I began to wonder if self-esteem was a product I could find in the canned goods aisle at my local grocery; peas, beans, corn, self-esteem, beets, pickles...

If only it were that easy! Over the years I have given a good deal of thought and contemplation to my mother's advice, and I wondered what letting someone "push my buttons" has to do with my self-esteem levels.

One day while driving down the road and listening to a tape by one of the leading authorities on self-esteem, I heard him say something that really stuck with me. I'll paraphrase here, but the core and heart of the matter was his contention that one of the worst things we can do to ourselves and our self–esteem is to utter the words, "Somehow I should know."

I pulled the car over. It was as though the skies opened up and manna from heaven was falling upon me. How often do we walk through a day thinking that thought? After all, as adults who have spent a certain amount of years on this planet, shouldn't we know? Shouldn't we know the right decisions to make, without having to be told? Our parents, teachers, ministers, and all other manner of authority figures taught us that, once we reached adulthood, *we should just know*. We should know the right decisions to make; what to say and what not to say; what to wear and what not to wear; how to discipline and reward children, coworkers, spouses; and generally what to do at every second of every day.

The truth is – and it may be tough to accept in this world of ours – that *you don't know everything*. Every time you tell yourself "Somehow I should know," you are doing yourself the worst kind of harm. You are belittling and impugning your own ability as a human being to function by supporting this impossible belief with your thinking, feelings and actions. You thereby diminish and destroy your self-esteem.

> It is absolutely nonsensical to believe that "somehow you should know" how to successfully manage one hundred percent of your life one hundred percent of the time. Instead, you should ask yourself: By whose standards am I measuring my success?

Please tell me if when you were born you were given life's manual. You know, it's the book you believe everyone else received. It spells out for you step by step every move you should make for every moment of your life. It explains in complete detail how you should prepare for adversity and how to handle it when it happens. It tells you how to raise perfect children and how to care for elderly parents. It even gives you a flow chart on how to best deal with that difficult boss who didn't tell you that his wife just left him and his children won't speak to him and he is waiting for his doctor to give him the results of his latest colonoscopy, opting instead to tell you what a terrible job you did on that project last week. You know the one: everyone else who looked at it regards it as the best work you've ever submitted. In fact it's the best work that anyone in the history of the company has ever submitted – but you laid awake last night because "somehow you should know" how to please your boss. Somehow you should know how you could have possibly done it any better.

That's ridiculous. It is absolutely nonsensical to believe that "somehow you should know" how to successfully manage one hundred percent of your life one hundred percent of the time. Instead, you should ask yourself, *By whose standards am I measuring my success?* The standards that live in your head because other people put them there? The standards that you strive to achieve when by golly they forgot to give you the book that everyone else received when they were born? The standards handed down by your parents, your preacher, your teacher, and all the rest of your life's overlords? It makes no sense to me that we continually do this evil thing to ourselves. I say it needs to stop now!

That is why I am writing a book on buttons – your buttons. I want us all to know how to recognize them and how to reset them. It's these buttons getting pushed everyday that cause our self-esteem to go spiraling out of control. Daniel Goleman, the author of *Emotional Intelligence*, refers to it as the "amygdala hijacking." It's when you actually have a chemical reaction in your brain that causes you to "see red" or even black out in extreme cases.

Some people refer to button pushing as Taking It Personally. You've heard it asked and may even have asked it yourself: *Why do you take things so personally?* I have something to tell you. You *are* a person. These things that you are Taking Personally are being said about you or about someone you love or about a project in which you invested yourself. You are *personally involved*, and it is only human to *take them personally*.

My goal is to teach you how to recognize when your buttons get pushed and to learn how to reset those buttons. I won't promise that the buttons aren't going to get pushed; that's life and life happens. We are expected to handle it. What may be keeping you from handling it well is the fact that you allow the old rule – *Somehow you should know* – to govern your reaction.

The first step in correcting this reaction is to question the rule. The very next time you hear those words in your head, stop and ask yourself why. Why *should* you know the correct answer, the appropriate response, the absolute right thing to do every single time? Why should you know, when you have never experienced the very next moment of your life before. How can you possibly know what to expect from that unknown moment or how to deal with it?

Can you remember when you bought your first house, met your best friend, saw your child for the first time? In remembering all of those first moments, ask yourself if there was any way you could possibly have known exactly what to do or how to react. Time changes everything; each individual moment changes what you know and the experience from which you draw the appropriate reaction. Even now, as you read this, you are taking in new information, changing your frame of reference and therefore changing you.

My mother taught me a great many things. I'm sure that yours did, too. We are all taught a great many lessons by those people older and wiser than ourselves. Many, if not most of these lessons are good ones, but there are some that we must unlearn if we hope to be emotionally healthy.

One of the lessons I have been trying to un-teach myself lately is that old axiom, "Somehow, you should know." I have been trying to reset my own buttons. In the following pages, I hope you will find a method of resetting that will work for you. Not everyone resets in the exact same way; what works for me won't work for you three-quarters of the time. Each individual person- ality reacts in a different way. My hope is that by using my RESET model, you will be able to find yourself in this book, and in turn be able to find a suitable way to reset. So if you're ready, let's go!

CHAPTER ONE: RECOGNITION

CHAPTER ONE: RECOGNITION

> Most people simply don't know why they're burned out. All they know is that they no longer want to do what they do ...

We as working people often have major problems with motivation, productivity and the ever-popular diagnosis of burnout. When asked why we've hit a slump in workplace output or have displayed a somewhat negative attitude, our first – and most of the time, honest – answer is, "I don't know."

This not knowing can sometimes be a source of desperation for those of us in high-pressure, high-expectation positions. Most people simply don't know why they're burned out. All they know is that they no longer want to do what they do for a living. But think about this:

One Monday you get in the car to go to work and it's a little harder to get the car up to speed than usual. On Tuesday you smell something burning, and by Wednesday the engine is burnt out. An entire tank of gas is gone when it usually takes you a week of city driving before you need to fill up. Something must be wrong with the car, so you take it to a mechanic, who is also baffled. Weeks go by, and because you don't have a car, you're not getting anywhere. Neither you nor your mechanic noticed that the emergency brake handle is pulled, and that you have been driving with it on for a week now.

The solution to the problem above should have been simple, shouldn't it? And yet the driver I just described will soon be on the hunt for a new car, even though her old one probably would be fixable upon diagnosis. What is the problem here? Our driver wasn't able to look for a cause – however simple – for her car's poor performance. She could not recognize that something which could cause her automobile to burn itself out had occurred, and failing to recognize that caused her car to burn out.

This scenario can easily be applied to what any driven person goes through in the workplace. No matter how strong-willed, how optimistic and positive, or how motivated you are, there are times when outside influences cause you difficulty and rob you of your enthusiasm for your work. Somebody or something has pushed your buttons, and you must reset. However, it does no good for you to learn how to reset your buttons if you do not recognize two things: first, that a button has indeed been pushed and second, what outside factor has pushed it.

In this chapter we'll examine the *R* in *RESET*: **R**ecognition.

The Volcanic Effect

> It is a volcanic effect: the build-up of pressure eventually causes an eruption of red-hot lava and you lash out …

A button getting pushed doesn't have to be a major monumental event. In fact, quite often that first button is pushed during a rather mundane occurrence or exchange. That little tiny mundane occurrence – because it really is so very insignificant, isn't it? – gets pushed aside, as does the next little tiny occurrence, and the next, and the next, until there's no room to put those button-pushers anymore. It is a volcanic effect: the build-up of pressure eventually causes an eruption of red-hot lava and you lash out – often at the very same type of little tiny mundane occurrence you had originally pushed aside.

So let's look at our volcano of internal reactions.

Physical Reaction

> When somebody says or does something that really pushes a button with us, our shoulder and neck muscles tighten. When a button gets pushed, our heart rate elevates.

The lowest or bottom section of the volcano is also the largest. That's because, as humans, we can internalize a great deal of outside stimuli and ignore those things which push our buttons. The key to recognizing those small stimuli at this stage of our internal volcano is through our minute physical reactions.

Have you ever heard the phrase, "Well, that really got his hackles up!"? Pet owners reading this recognize when their cat or dog feels threatened, because the skin and hair around their shoulders and the back of their necks – their *hackles* – raise and the fur puffs out. This physical reaction is mainly a visual effect; it is naturally designed to make the animal look bigger and more threatening, in order to frighten off whatever animal is threatening it.

But in humans that reaction occurs physically, as well. When somebody says or does something that really pushes a button with us, our shoulder and neck muscles tighten. Chiropractors and massage therapists speak of "storing stress"; that is, we store stress in our necks, shoulders, upper backs and pectoral muscles. We tighten those muscles up the tiniest bit when a button gets pushed, but we don't release. The next time a button gets pushed, we tighten those muscles up even more. We don't release. Before long, we can't get comfortable, can't relax, lose sleep, and experience headaches.

Another physical reaction which occurs is also animalistic in nature. When a button gets pushed, our heart rate elevates. Fight-or-flight kicks in, and our hearts literally beat faster than normal in anticipation of some conflict or in preparation for an escape. As with muscle tightening, this happens gradually and incrementally. It's not as if we go from 100 beats per minute to 225 in the space of a second; mid-level executives would arrive in the hospital with cardiac arrests at the rate of five per minute. But your heart does begin to work harder and your adrenaline does release, making you more edgy, more prone to overreact to outside stimuli, especially unfavorable stimuli.

Confusion

The next section in our volcano of internal reactions is *Confusion*.

> Quite often in the workplace, we are confronted with situations that confuse us because our personal value systems don't include activities we witness or attitudes we experience.

A business colleague once told me a story about change that helps to illustrate what I mean by confusion. I'm not talking about change in the sense of changing your route to work, or the kind of car you drive, I'm talking about pocket change. Paul was in a meeting with several coworkers, and at the end of that meeting one of them asked him for three dollars for the bus. Not having any ones in his wallet, Paul simply gave the coworker five dollars. The two of them left their office building and went their separate ways. Over his shoulder Paul saw his coworker approached by a person begging for change. To his disbelief, he overheard the coworker say, "No, I don't have any extra money."

The mathematics of the situation imply that Paul's coworker did indeed have extra money; he needed three dollars for the bus and received five, giving him an extra *two dollars*, out of which a quarter or two would probably not be missed. This was Paul's thinking, anyway. Incensed, he approached his coworker and asked him very pointedly about his refusal to give the beggar some change. His response? "It's my money."

Paul tried to point out the fact that it was, in fact, *his* money all too recently. He didn't understand his coworker's set of values regarding possession, ownership and charity. What his coworker had done *confused* Paul, because it didn't jibe with Paul's worldview.

Quite often in the workplace, we are confronted with situations that confuse us because our personal value systems don't include activities we witness or attitudes we experience. This confusion *pushes our buttons*; it causes us to question our surroundings and, if the answers to our questions are not satisfactory, can trigger frustration and anger which block out sensible thought and judgment.

The other major form of confusion we find in the workplace is what I call the **persecution confusion**.

Persecution confusion can be summed up most easily with the phrase, "Why are they doing this *to me*?" It is the feeling of being singled out, the feeling of helplessness and powerlessness, and the lack of understanding as to why you are being treated so poorly. That feeling of persecution, of helplessness can be just as powerful and just as vision-clogging as frustration and rage. "Why should I even do my work," you might think, "if everybody else is just going to undermine it?"

We often hear the phrase "deer-in-the-headlights" used to describe a person who has been caught off guard. Deer, opossums and other nocturnal animals see oncoming headlights and the brightness and directness of the beams both frightens and confuses them. Although logic might tell you to get out of the way of an oncoming mass much larger than yourself, instinct takes over in instances of fright and confusion. Instinct tells any animal – humans included – that movement is dangerous. Predators notice movement. Instinct tells animals to remain still so that the predator will not attack.

This happens in pushed-button situations that involve value confusion and persecution confusion as well. It is only natural when this confusion button gets pushed that you should think, "I don't know what to do. I'm confused and this situation isn't making sense to me. I'll just stay still." In this case, instinct may be natural, but it can also be deadly. Let's not forget what happens to the deer or the opossum that gets "caught in the headlights": eventually the car hits them.

<u>Overwhelm</u>

So these first two levels of the volcano have been activated. You have your initial physical reaction before you even realize that a button has been pushed. That subconscious reaction happens first, and then the realization of your confusion occurs. A button has been pushed! And we all know what happens when we actually realize that we have been wronged: our emotions kick in, and "amygdala hijackings" occur.

> You are not alone, and you don't have to be a robot to get through it. You are allowed to feel.

There is no shortage of feelings that can rush through us all at once when a button gets pushed. Our behavioral styles determine our reactions, but at one point or another we have all felt the following emotions:

Anger
Annoyance
Confusion
Concern
Disappointment
Discouragement
Distress
Fright
Frustration
Helplessness
Hopelessness
Impatience
Irritation
Loneliness
Nervousness
Overwhelm
Puzzlement
Reluctance
Sadness
Discomfort

Wow! That's certainly a long list of emotions! And believe it or not, when a button gets pushed and you get to that third level of the volcano, the likelihood is that you'll feel more, not less of those emotions in turn or, worse, all at once. The inevitable result of buttons being pushed – and feeling annoyance, nervousness, anger and fear all at once – is the only 'O' on our list: *Overwhelm*.

Failure to recognize that buttons are being pushed can cause confusion, emotions and physical reactions all to pile up. Your mind, body and heart are all going in so many directions that they can't even cooperate with themselves, let alone with each other. Believe it or not, everyone feels like this. You are not alone, and you don't have to be a robot to get through it. You are allowed to feel.

This overwhelm can cause volcanic eruptions: behavioral reactions which are undesirable on the low end, and which on the high end are absolutely mortifying and can be detrimental to your relationships at work and at home. But different people act, react and act out in different ways. It is important, if you are unable to recognize the initial systems that begin your own underground rumblings, that you are able to recognize your own "act-out" moments.

One division among people during eruptions has to do with volume. When your buttons are pushed, do you get loud, or do you get quiet? Neither is desirable; ask anyone who has been on the receiving end of "The Silent Treatment" whether being yelled at is worse than being ignored. Some people yell and scream and hurl epithets at others, whether those others pushed their buttons or simply walked into the room at the wrong time. Other people get very quiet, very introverted, and shut everyone around them out. Both of these re-actions are defense mechanisms designed to keep out any potentially hurtful stimuli: the loud person drowns them out, while the quiet person refuses to acknowl-edge them.

What about yourself? Are you a person who en-gages others in confrontation when your buttons are pushed? Or are you a person who withdraws from in-teraction when your volcano finally erupts?

Your behavioral reactions can have significant im-pact not just on your personal and professional relation-ships, but via those relationships your career and well-being – both physical and financial – can be negatively affected. Most people do not recognize the warning signs – the first three layers of their personal volcanoes – and the resulting eruptions give them reputations for being difficult to work with: "He's sulky." "She goes off at the slightest thing!"

So keep our volcanic components in mind as you go through your day. Take inventory of yourself as you go through your day. Have you experienced any of the physical reactions – muscle tightening, quickening of breath and heartbeat – that are coincidental with a pushed button? Have you found yourself questioning the motivations of others, as if you are being punished or persecuted for an unknown reason? Go through our list of emotions. Are you feeling any of these, or a combination of them? Do you recognize any of the warning signs of an eruption?

An important thing to remember as you go through your day and as you take a self-inventory is that *these reactions are normal and natural.* Each and every human being feels some of these mental, physical and emotional reactions almost each and every day. The key to RESETting is that you recognize these reactions as indicators of a pushed button – *early* – rather than as symptoms that led up to an eruption – *too late.*

> Are you a person who engages others in confrontation when your buttons are pushed? Or are you a person who withdraws from interaction when your volcano finally erupts?

CHAPTER TWO: EXPECTATIONS

Chapter Two: Expectations

> Disappointment breeds where there is no opportunity.

Why are our buttons pushed? In many instances the answer is a simple case of expectations not being met. After all, the most fundamental confusion can be broken down as being that between what happens and what we expect to happen. Our expectations are at the core of our values, beliefs, the way we think and feel, and in the end, our behavior. Expectations are, at their heart, ways in which we set ourselves up for disappointment. We expect something to occur, it does not, and we are disappointed. This chapter is as much about resetting the *disappointment* button as it is about resetting the *expectation* button.

We behave in accordance with our expectations of the way events *will* or *should* transpire, and with our expectations of the way things *are*. We act in accordance with our expectations of the way others *will* or *should* behave, as well as the way *we ourselves* will or should behave. When those expectations are not met – or, in many cases, are flat out contradicted – we experience a fundamental confusion that pushes our second-level button. Translation: *we are disappointed*. Disappointment breeds anger and frustration. The lava in our personal volcanoes rises to a level that should begin creating alarm in the population that surrounds us.

Disappointment breeds where there is no opportunity. Our expectations cannot be met when there is no opportunity for them to be met, or when that opportunity is missed or ignored. Think about it: disappointment truly arises from the "woulda-shoulda-coulda's" of life. We expect buses and planes to be on time so that we can get where we need to be in a punctual fashion. We need projects to be completed. We need applause at the end of an event, a simple thank-you for a job well done, and peace at the end of the day. When these simplest of expectations are not or cannot be met, the *expectation* button has been pressed.

We have already discussed ways to recognize when these buttons are being pushed; that is, we are now able to recognize that our expectations are not being met, as well as to anticipate the negative physical and behavioral outcomes of that disappointment. What I'd like to do in this chapter is one method of preventing those disappointment buttons from being pushed by resetting a button that was pushed a long, long time ago.

We need to reset the "NO" button.

> We didn't know what we didn't know until we were told no.

When we were children, we heard the word *no* a lot. A University of California at Los Angeles survey found that the average one-year-old hears the word "no" more than 400 times a day. Those of you who have children probably heard it spouted back to you as one of your child's first words. We heard *no* because we were curious and because we were small, and because we touched and pulled down and explored and tore up things that we were not supposed to. We didn't know our boundaries. We didn't know what we didn't know until we were told *no*.

The problem with all of this *no*-ing is that we grew to detest hearing the word said. Hearing *no* began to elicit an emotional rather than a practical or disciplinary reaction. This wasn't a rejection of our request, it was a rejection of *us*, and it hurt. We did all that we could to avoid it. We learned to play word games or to bargain, or we learned to simply take or do without asking. So powerful is this aversion to the word *no* that we still try to avoid it as adults! And in doing so, we fail to make requests.

"I don't fail to make requests, Mary Elizabeth!" you say. "I ask for things all the time!"

What many people fail to realize is that simply asking for something is different from making a request. The difference lies in the requester's implied willingness to hear *no*. Many of us do not have this willingness. We are not so giving and open-hearted that we are willing to concede that somebody may not be willing to meet our expectations. This fact frustrates us, especially if the person we ask is *able* but not *willing* to do as we request.

I would like to outline in this chapter some methods of request that are doomed from their outset. These are requests that either poison the deal or poison your relationship with the person you're asking, or worse: *both*.

The Weak Favor

The first – and probably most common – form of doomed request is the *favor*. A favor is a soft, weak request that begs the requested to say no, or, more likely, to find some excuse not to follow through. The favor request usually begins in one of the following ways:

"I need…" or "Could you do me a favor…?"
"Can you help me out – I'll owe you one…?"
"It would be nice if…?"

The major fault in all of these forms of request is that they suggest an imposition on the part of the requester and create a feeling of obligation or guilt on the part of the requestee. While you do expect that the other person will reply in the affirmative, you are also expecting them to *accommodate* you. They feel manipulated; they feel that they are responding to an authority outside of themselves.

Stock replies – *which may go unspoken!* – among those who deny your favor requests may include:

"I might…but I'm not going to!"
"I can, but I won't."
"Yep. Sure would be nice."

Why do people reply in these ways? Because of the tone of your request. By phrasing it as a favor to you, you give the other person license to infer that doing you that favor will somehow cost them their time, effort and energy, all of which could have been spent doing something else. The "favor tone" can also imply that the requested task is one you could complete yourself, but which is something that you don't feel like doing. And if you don't want to do it yourself, why in the world would anyone else want to do it *for* you?

> The feeling they get ... is that you are using your position or your relationship with them so that they will do your dirty work for you.

Even if your friend, colleague or family member does accommodate your favor request, the aftermath may be poisoned just a bit. You may have pushed *their* buttons. How did you do this? Well, no matter how you phrase your favor request, your implication is "If you really are my friend/a good coworker/a loving relative, you'll do this for me so that I don't have to."

The feeling they get — as they begrudgingly carry out your request, all the while grumbling to themselves — is that you are *using* your position or your relationship with them so that they will do your dirty work for you. By not leaving the door open for your counterpart to say "no," you have dropped just enough poison in the well to leave a bad taste in his or her mouth.

The Demand

Believe it or not, many folks in the working world define *request* as *telling somebody to do something*. This couldn't be further from the truth. You are truly closing the door on *no* and locking away the key here. This is not a request; it is a demand. When saying no is explicitly deleted from the list of options – rather than *implicitly*, as described with the favor – then a request becomes a demand.

The trouble with making a demand rather than a true request is, of course, that doing so is unreasonable. It is not reasonable to assume that another person's schedule will be able to accommodate your needs, and it is not reasonable to demand that they rearrange things to meet your "request." Demands often start in the following ways:

"Do this."

"I'm going to need you to…"

"You need to…"

"You're required to…"

"You have to…"

"Because I said so."

"You want to…" or "Tell Mary to…"

Not only do these phrases deny an answer of *no*, they deny the other person the chance to say anything at all. Since they perceive that there are no options beyond carrying out the task demanded, there is no reason to respond to the demand itself. Closing down communication like this is perhaps the most dangerous thing you can do in terms of your relationships with others. If others feel they cannot communicate with you, they will avoid approaching you. Resentments build up. *More and more buttons get pushed.*

In this way, you have set the situation up for inevitable failure. Your colleague/relative/friend will respond in one of two ways to a demand. They might flat-out refuse to carry out your demand. This not only builds up resentment in you – pushing your expectation button – but also slows down your day, as you *expected* the task to be completed. This pushes your panic button as well. Now you are behind schedule, certain benchmarks won't be reached because the necessary steps have not been taken, and your reputation will suffer. This pushes your time button, your failure button and your self- and other-image buttons, all at the same time. You are also pushing the other person's *control* button. Who is in control of the situation and of the relationship is now being contested. And if you want to measure the amount of time until your next eruption after all that, you'd better have a second hand on your watch.

On the other hand, the person you've demanded to do this task may, in fact, complete the task. All is well, right? Well, in fact, the resentment that will have built up in this person has done more than just leave a sour taste in his or her mouth. This resentment has truly poisoned the well, and repeated demands of this nature are going to make sure that loyalty and respect from your colleagues disappears, and that your friends become passing acquaintances in short order.

The Mind-Reading Request

All of us who have been in a long-term relationship know a little something about telepathy. Either we can read our significant others' minds, or they wish we could and expect us to. A major pet peeve of mine is when people do not request gifts for birthdays or the holidays. *They should know what I want*, these people think, *I shouldn't have to tell them*.

While fiction, television and the movies may tell you differently, other people cannot read your mind. The non-request request – that is, relying on other people to know you so well that they know what you want instinctually – is on the opposite end of the spectrum from the demand. Rather than telling your colleague exactly what you want and giving him or her no way to tell you no, you tell your colleague nothing, giving them little or no way to accommodate you. Once again you set yourself up for failure, since the only way to succeed is to literally imbue your counterpart with ESP.

> Your requests are fair to make, and it is not reasonable for you to assume that others know what you're thinking or feeling.

So how does this failure push your expectation button? Quite simply, the mind-reading request is a symptom of unrealistic expectations. It is also a symptom both of a deflated sense of self and an inflated sense of what others think of you.

The mind-reading request is symptomatic of the deflated sense of self insofar as you, the requester, feel guilty about making a request in the first place. You feel that you're imposing upon the other person, or that your request is not really a *need*, but rather a *want*. On the other hand, your sense of others' perception of you is inflated, because you think that they should know what you want without your telling them. You imagine that others focus an inordinate amount of energy on reading your mood, reading your feelings and observing subtle signals you give out. In fact, neither of these perceptions are true. Your requests *are* fair to make, and it is *not* reasonable for you to assume that others know what you're thinking or feeling. By behaving this way you are actually reinforcing the "somehow you should know" falsehood.

The Suggestive Request

The following request attempt is one of my favorites, because we do it so unconsciously. One version of the mind-reading request that is more prevalent among long-term couples than with co-workers is the suggestive request. The suggestive request might sound like this: "I'm thirsty."

What is your significant other supposed to do with this? What you want is for them to get you something to drink, but you're not asking them to do that. What you are doing is telling them how you feel. You're asking them to assume that you want them to take a certain action based on your feeling. In essence, you're *assuming* that they will assume your expectation and act on that assumption. That's very shaky ground to stand on. After all, what if their assumption is *wrong?*

Reasonable Requests

> You have to be willing to hear no.

So, if our most common forms of request are faulty at their root, what is the best way to request a favor, service or action from another person? Quite simply, you have to be willing to let them deny that request. You have to be willing to hear *no*.

Straightforward requests are the best. Our unwillingness to hear *no* causes us to dance around the crux of the matter, to try to fool the person we're asking into saying *yes* when they don't want to. Reasonable requests take into account the other person's desires and abilities as well as our own. They are clear, concise, and free of cajoling, conniving, or trickery.

A straightforward request can be phrased like this:

"Would you be willing to…?"
"Will you…?"
"Is it feasible for you to…?"
"Are you willing to…? How willing are you? How likely is it that you would be willing to…?"

Phrasing your requests this way provides a direct opposite to asking someone if they *want* to do something, or if they *can* do something. These types of requests take into account that the other person may not be able to accommodate them, or that they may not want to do so, or both. More importantly on a personal level, they do not *assume* anything.

A reasonable request is one that pushes *no* buttons. Your counterpart does not feel obligated or forced to do anything for you, and you in turn have mitigated any unrealistic expectations that you may have by preparing to hear them say *no*. In the end, other people will be more likely to grant your requests in the future, even if they are unable or unwilling to do so now, simply because you're willing to hear the word *no*.

Remember, *no* doesn't always mean never; sometimes it just means "not now," or "let's negotiate." More importantly, most times "no" creates an opportunity to clarify, adjust and align expectations.

CHAPTER THREE:
SENSE OF SELF

Chapter Three: Sense of Self

> Our sense of self governs our reactions to others'
> behavior as much as – if not more than –
> our expectations.

In the previous chapter, we discussed our expectations insofar as the way we want things to happen and the way we want other people to act. We touched upon the way unfulfilled expectations push our buttons and how we can react to those buttons being pushed.

Analyzing expectations involves examining external influences upon our mood, our view of the world and our behavior in response to those external events. That is, we react based on the way we see the world. But what about the way we see ourselves? Our sense of self governs our reactions to others' behavior as much as – if not more than – our expectations.

Your sense of self is ultimately influenced by your internal drivers. No matter which behavioral style you adhere to most, your internal drivers are the same as any other person's: your needs, your values and beliefs, your thoughts, and your feelings ultimately drive *your actions*. These internal drivers do not change unless a significant emotional event occurs – a divorce, loss of a loved one, major promotion or change in financial status, etc. – as an internal motivator which provokes the change. These things drive everything; when we speak about external influences, it is needs, values, thoughts and feelings about which we are speaking. We view and perceive our external world through the lens of these internal drivers.

Here's an absolute for you: *It is never advisable to work in absolutes*. Avoid classifying a person as either Type-A or Type-B, as either serene or disagreeable, as an introvert or an extrovert. Every person is different, and every behavioral style is made up of a unique blend of tendencies, expectations and perceptions. In the language of RESET, no person has just one button. We all have a switchboard which includes several different buttons. Some buttons, however, are larger than others. Let's focus on four buttons which tend to be the largest on most people's switchboards.

The Accomplishment Button

The *accomplishment* button gets pushed most in people who are driven by their achievements and who like to control their own destinies through those achievements. Let's say that there exists a person ruled only by his or her accomplishment button. Such a person would order and schedule his or her life from goal to goal, with the bar set higher and higher for each consecutive achievement. The quality of reward is raised with each accomplishment, but so is the degree of intensity needed to attain it.

Soon, Accomplishment Button folks are demanding this level of intensity not only from themselves, but from those who work with them as well. When they don't sense that their coworkers are working up to snuff, the Accomplishment Button gets pushed and pushed hard. Three reactions occur, each – like their personal work drive – increasing in intensity. They will get loud, physically displaying their frustration with intimidating and demanding behavior.

The first reaction many driven people have is to lash out. It's a loud verbal outburst, occasionally accompanied by the "pointing finger." *Why didn't you...* is a common outburst phrasing. Another is *I thought I told you to...* What's usually the final lash-out is one we've all heard before from driven people: *I guess I'll have to take care of this myself.*

This type of outburst often leads directly to the second level of Accomplishment Button eruption: *doing it all by yourself.* Many driven people are of the "If you want things done ..." mentality, and if their expectations are not met will begin taking on tasks and responsibilities previously assigned to others. This can be detrimental to a workplace, friendly or home environment for several reasons.

First, the people whose responsibilities are being taken away from them were assigned those duties for a reason. They have expertise or at the very least experience with those tasks and have demonstrated proficiency at them. Taking the tasks upon yourself disrupts the flow and efficiency of your environment. This action is destructive to interpersonal relationships as well. Imagine it being implied that you are so bad at your job that a person who has a million other things on his or her plate can take it away from you and do it better. That's insulting, and will be met with resistance and eventually an overall lack of cooperation.

The final eruption caused by inability to reset the Accomplishment Button is *burnout.* We have all heard the term before, but it's thrown around quite loosely nowadays. It should not be. Burnout is a serious problem in today's workplace and is just what it sounds like. A person, no matter how driven, has worked so hard for so long that his or her mental and emotional gears are simply burnt out. Unlike the car engine, however, many of these gears may not be replaceable. It becomes impossible to focus on the task at hand and impossible to find any motivation to continue doing what they're doing. In short, burning out is becoming the opposite of what accomplishment people want to be, and burnout begets burnout. An accomplishment motto might be "what do we need to do – and who can I get to do it?"

The Recognition Button

For some people, the most important thing is that they receive accolades for their accomplishments, that they are recognized for what they do. In these people, the Recognition Button is primary. This is not to say that they live only for recognition. Rather, Recognition Button folks like to know that what they've done has had an effect on the world around them. Whereas driven Accomplishment Button people get their greatest reward from reaching their goals, Recognition Button people derive their satisfaction from knowing that their hard work has influenced those around them.

They gain this understanding through public acknowledgement and, in some cases, reward.

This large kind of recognition is usually reserved for reaching the end of a project or meeting a goal or milestone. But Recognition Button people need accolades along the way, too, and receive it through the approval of others in the form of friendship and popularity. Nothing tells you that you influence those around you like the reputation and characteristics of the "social butterfly." A belief for those with a high recognition button is "It's not what you know but who you know – and who knows you."

Recognition people have a high need to be liked, to be everybody's friend and enjoy a work environment that encourages teamwork, a good deal of free interaction and creative approaches to work-related problems. The high-energy environment this behavioral style enjoys fosters a warm and caring atmosphere, reinforced through its encouragement of social interaction, impromptu meetings and brainstorming sessions, and an overall sense of high passion for the work the company is doing.

As we did before, let us imagine a person who is entirely and completely driven by his or her Recognition Button. This person would do everything he or she did for the sake of being praised for it later. If a day went by when this person was not applauded, did not receive a trophy, was not asked to stand up and be counted, the Recognition Button would be pushed. Reminds you of one or two pop stars who've been in the news, doesn't it?

Luckily, as with accomplishment people – and all other behavioral styles, as a matter of fact – it is very rare that a person exists who has only one button. But in a person *primarily* driven by the Recognition Button, the fear of being ignored can grow to be so great that he or she may "act out," attempting to garner attention through any means necessary. When the *lack of recognition* button has been pushed the reaction is that of a tantrum -- stamping feet, flailing arms, a loud, interruptive voice or over talking.

A lack of public recognition – a company party, awards ceremony, or organization-wide memo – can eventually lead to resentment and withdrawal from business functions. Eventually, folks who have a more sensitive Recognition Button may pull away from work itself, feeling that anything they accomplish simply is not worth it if nobody's going to pay attention to their achievements.

The Stability Button

> The one thing in this crazy world that we can completely control is our connection to it.

Up until now, we have dealt in our hypothetical "one-button" studies with people whose buttons compelled them to value improving their situations above everything else. That is, these folks are interested in being at the center of change within their organizations. But there is another button within all of us that seeks what is comfortable, what is familiar, and favors the known over the unknown. We call that the *stability* button.

If you think of our internal buttons as release valves, you can understand the thought process of a person for whom the stability button is primary. Imagine again a hypothetical person with only a stability button. The more things change, the more uncertainty is entered into the situation in which that person finds him or herself, the more that button is going to get pushed. "Release the pressure," our stability person begs, "Release it now before I crack!"

If your only button is stability, you might be driven by appreciation like a recognition person, but that appreciation needs to come in the form of personal congratulation. A big party is too much, and may read as insincere to you. A personal and intimate "thank you" is much more valuable in your mind. It allows you to feel appreciated, but not in a way that is going to disrupt your day.

Workers with Stability Buttons primarily value a work environment based around cooperation, humility, and a team-first ethic. They quietly contemplate and consider the consequences of actions taken, and expect their co-workers to do the same; risk-takers are not appreciated. Challenges are met with resistance, because it may be seen as unnecessary change and it might be better to set smaller goals along the road to a huge test rather than expecting them to pass it all at once. A motto for people with a stability button could be "Measure twice, cut once."

Stability people need to know that everything is going to be all right. When they find themselves in situations where everything works as planned, where everything goes smoothly and all of the trains run on time, naturally they would fear anything that threatens that status quo. So our hypothetical stability-only worker might go through several stages of eruption, much like our hypothetical accomplishment-only worker.

The first step in this eruption is going to be withdrawal. Stability folks don't want to rock the boat, whether that boat belongs to them or to their co-workers. They cherish constancy and harmony over all else. Therefore, they are not going to throw a tantrum or yell at anyone. There will be no outward eruption; rather, their reaction is going to be much more like an ulcer, something that bubbles up inside for so long that eventually it eats away from the inside. Therefore stability folks will withdraw, going inside and eventually cutting off from interpersonal contact in order to alleviate pressure. After all, the one thing in this crazy world that we can completely control is our connection to it.

The problem, of course, is that no one can keep that kind of stress and internal pressure under wraps for too long. Eventually it can bubble out unexpectedly in the form of poor or erratic work, coldness or rudeness towards family and co-workers, and sometimes in the form of physical ailments which develop from mental and emotional stress.

The Correctness Button

The *correctness* button is large in most people, and it has a hair trigger. It's set off by criticism, by second-guessing and by ill-informed decision-making. It's the primary button for conscientious and detail-oriented workers, and it causes the quickest reactions when hit.

Quite simply, correctness people are driven by their need to be right about absolutely everything.

Don't misunderstand. Correctness folks don't insist that they are right and that you are wrong and accept no evidence to the contrary. When I say that they must be right about everything, what I mean is that they don't want to give themselves the chance to be wrong. They research every problem, every aspect of a project, every possible twist or turn to a story thoroughly. They refuse to give themselves the option of getting any detail incorrect.

The intense fear of being wrong is not a pride thing. Correctness Button people are afraid that if they are incorrect about something, then the consequences for their work environment, their project, or their families could be dire. In order to achieve this end, correctness people are typically quiet, methodical workers who put as much effort into the preparation as they do into creating the finished product.

Our hypothetical worker with only a correctness button to his name would be right at home in a work environment where quality and dependability are prized above risk-taking or the fast-paced product push. Inconsistency and impulsiveness are huge button-pushers for our correctness worker. "Going with your gut" is unacceptable to him, as he insists upon a more logic-based approach to all things. There is a cynicism towards new ideas if those ideas are untested. Make no mistake: the risk-reward ratio with correctness people is always going to favor the reward. Most people with the correctness button are focused on the task at hand – an often heard phrase from one of my favorite correctness people is "I do one thing. I do it very well and then I move on."

As you can tell, the Correctness Button can in many cases be very easily pushed. That's because in a healthy and prosperous work environment new ideas are constantly invented, suggested and put into at least limited use before they have been one hundred percent proven. This can be where eruption begins. But be careful: it's not one that can easily be detected.

Correctness folks tend to "withdraw with dignity." They don't want to cause a big scene, don't want to react to poor logic illogically. After all, what would be the point? Such a reaction would only perpetuate an already "out-of-control" situation.

So folks with a gigantic Correctness Button withdraw from the situation. Their reaction is much like stability people, with the exception that emotion completely disappears from the equation. While stability people react with fear and resentment which causes them to internalize, correctness people would try to suppress those emotions as also illogical.

When pushed, the next stage of the eruption is to attack with facts. And make no mistake: they have the facts! Due to their drive for correctness and their fear of criticism, people with this tendency will leave no stone unturned in their preparation to prove themselves "right."

Your Buttons

Observe your own behavior. How do you react in these situations? To what do you react most negatively?

As you read this chapter, my hope is that with each of these big four buttons you reacted the same way: "Oh, I do that...that must be me...hey, wait...maybe *that's* me!"

The point, of course, is that these four buttons – and hundreds of others – exist within each and every one of us. In each of us some buttons are larger or more sensitive than others, and therefore each of us reacts differently to different stimuli, based on our dominant behavioral style. Observe your own behavior. How do you react in these situations? To what do you react most negatively?

Come away from this chapter knowing that in order to truly Reset Your Buttons you must trust in the adages "Know thyself" and "To thy own self be true."

CHAPTER FOUR:

EMPHASIZE CORE VALUES

CHAPTER FOUR: EMPHASIZE CORE VALUES

> Quite simply, The Saboteur wants to knock you off-balance and change your focus ...

So now that we have recognized our individual buttons and taken stock of our Sense of Self, we should be fine, right? A button gets pushed, and we recognize that pushing for what it is, recognize the *button* for what it is, and we move on. Oh, if only it were that simple.

Unfortunately, as anyone who has made reference to a "guilty pleasure" knows, there's one last hurdle to overcome before we can truly begin to RESET.

Because our buttons are pre-wired for certain reactions, those reactions are the easy ones. We don't have to think about them, nor do we really have to put forth any extra effort in order to react. We simply do it in-stinctively; everyone knows that lashing out is easier than reasoning.

The truly difficult thing about the **RESET *Mindset*** is that even when we recognize our buttons and realize that pre-wired reactions are not necessarily the best or most appropriate for a particular situation, they are still the *easiest* reactions to have. We hear that little voice in our heads telling us to go the easy route, to do what we "want" to do, rather than what is the most appropriate thing to do.

That's the voice of The Saboteur.

The Saboteur wants you to take the easy path. The Saboteur wants you to have the negative reaction, to blow up, or withdraw, or throw a tantrum, or overwork. Quite simply, The Saboteur wants to knock you off-bal-ance and change your focus from the *ultimate goal* to the *immediate release*. Everybody has his or her own Sabo-teur. Mine happens to look like The Noid: that evil little red guy who destroyed pizzas in the commercials back in the '80s. Yours may be a gremlin, or a taunting child, or your mother-in-law. Whatever form *It* takes, all Saboteurs are after one thing and one thing only: they want you to be miserable, and they will achieve this goal by stealing your greatness!

The Saboteur, playing the role of bodyguard, appears to want to protect you. Wherever there exists the possibility of even a single negative consequence to your actions, there *It* stands, in the path of your making that decision. The Saboteur is a cunning manipulator; *It* even whispers to you in your own voice. You may have heard yourself saying something like:

"If I take that job, I'll have to move. I might not see my family as often. I don't want to be separated from my parents and siblings."

"If I go back to school, I may incur debt, and there's no guarantee that a job will be waiting for me when I finally do graduate. Heck, I might not even graduate!"

"If I go up on the roof to fix the antenna, I might fall down and break my neck! I don't really need to see the game clearly, do I?"

Now, it's understandable that many of you no longer have television antennae on the roof of your home, but you grasp my point. The Saboteur pretends to protect, but in actuality *It prevents*. It prevents us from reaching our goals by implying that the steps which must be taken to reach those goals are too dangerous. *It* encourages us to take the easy path rather than take a risk. *It* can accomplish all of this because *It* has been living inside each and every one of us for a long time, and *It* understands the values we hold dear. In all that time, The Saboteur has certainly learned to hijack those values.

What do I mean by "hijacking values"? When a value is hijacked, your internal Saboteur uses your worldview against you in order to keep you from your goals. I often use the following example, one that affects nearly everyone.

Like many business owners, I work all the time. The term "nine-to-five" doesn't ring true to me, because I begin work upon waking and often work long into the wee morning hours of the next day. I work on Saturdays on a frequent basis. Sundays are the only days that I reserve for myself; those are days when I absolutely will not work. The body and the mind both need to recharge, and Sunday is my day to do that. That is an important core value of mine.

Another value that I hold is that of commitment and dependability. My clients deserve the work they hire me to do to be completed on time and in a satisfactory manner. Because I work on projects for clients, and because those projects are often on a deadline, I sometimes feel the urge to work on my day off -Sunday. If my portion of a client's project is due to that client on Wednesday, and I have not completed it on Saturday, that little red Noid pops up in my head, unlawfully riding my commitment and dependability value. It begins "should-ing on me." "You *should* work today," says the Noid. "Your project is not complete. You are unreliable. You are letting down your client."

> When a value is hijacked, your internal Saboteur uses your worldview against you in order to keep you from your goals.

He has hijacked one of my core values, that of being reliable and accountable, in order to sabotage another of my core values of resting and recharging on Sundays. My Saboteur is using my desire to provide the best possible service to my clients to lower the priority of rest for myself. "Stop being selfish," he says. "Your health and well-being is not as important as delivering good service to your clients. You can sacrifice a nap or an afternoon sipping lemonade if it means that their project is complete on time." It is a sneaky little demon that twists up one value in order to sabotage the other which quite often results in it sabotaging the entire outcome – ultimately leaving me feeling miserable!

How do I possibly combat that onslaught? The Noid is right. I'm being selfish, taking time for myself and therefore taking time away from my clients. Do I really need to watch that Sandra Bullock romantic comedy that I missed in the theatres or that NASCAR race with my husband? Do I really need to spend that hour on the phone with my sister? Wouldn't it help my client out if I put an afternoon into the job they hired me to do by Wednesday, instead of into my garden?

There are two ways to deal with the Saboteur. The first – and the most common, since he is a sneaky little bugger – is to give in. The Saboteur is very convincing, very manipulative. All too often his argument seems flawless, and in fact he makes our core values – those principles, morals, standards, ethics and ideals on which we base our *lives* – seem silly and inconsequential. He has us ready to abandon any endeavor upon which we embark.

But please realize that the Saboteur does not care which value he hijacks. If my core value was to *work* on Sunday, he would most assuredly hijack some other value in order to get me to take the day off. That little Noid is a liar, plain and simple. He is a liar whose sole purpose is to sabotage your greatness!

The second way to deal with the Saboteur is to get him to shut up. This is not easy to do, but it is possible. The Noid, the devil on your shoulder, the voice in your head; all of these Saboteurs use the same weapon: logical argument. They edit together your past mistakes and failures to create a horror-film version of your future. Saboteurs *convince* you that your desired course of action is the wrong one to take, the path most difficult, the path most frightening.

The best way to beat them is to realize that *you* are not your Saboteur but instead have become its *observer*. Re-emphasize your core values. Remind yourself *why* they are your core values, values which cannot be changed because they are the cornerstone of your life. Remove the stories of negativity and replace them with true accounts of your success. Pay attention to the generalities that *It* likes to use and counter with the specific facts of the situation.

When my Noid begins poking at me in the middle of a Sunday morning, I feel the pressure to work. But then I remind myself why I made resting on Sunday a core value. Beyond my basic religious upbringing, I chose to abstain from working for one day a week because my brain needs time to recharge. I remind myself that without that day of rest, without that time to relax, reflect and reboot, the quality of my work goes down drastically. What good is getting a project to a client on time, or a column into an editor on deadline, or math homework to your teacher on time, if that project or column or math homework is riddled with mistakes or simply below the standards it should meet?

Simply put, if my Saboteur convinces me to work when I shouldn't, the results may very well be so poor as to be unusable. My client would then have to start at least a portion of the project over again. Worse yet, my chances of having a long-term relationship with that client would have severely dropped, let alone my chances of a healthy long-term relationship with myself and my family.

> Do you know what your core values are?

When we re-emphasize our core values and observe – rather than react to – the Saboteur, we are better able to live by our own core values and thus maintain a level head. The old me would have given in to the Noid and worked on Sunday. The old me would have forgotten – like a Cubs fan who forgets that the Bartman ball wouldn't even have been the final out of the *inning*, let alone the *game* – that a project incomplete after Saturday but due on Wednesday could still be completed on time.

Emphasizing core values seems simple enough, and it can be. But do you know what your core values are? It's a strange question to ask, but a fair one. Many of us would be surprised if we sat down to dinner and were asked by a date, "So, what are your core values?" without time to prepare. It helps to make a list. Know exactly what your core values are, and be clear as to your guideposts for value-oriented living.

Now that you have your list in front of you, you're ready to combat the Saboteur. This is difficult, because he's stealthy, a sneak-attacker. By the time you know that something's wrong he's not just pushing your buttons, he's jumping up and down on them. There doesn't seem to be any feasible way to recover, because the little stinker's feet are about to come down on the button you just reset and he's pushing several of them at once.

However, it's still possible to take stock of what is happening with your buttons, if you take a moment to exhale. When you relax, take a moment and exhale, you create a cushion of air that – temporarily, at least – prevents the Saboteur from jumping up and down quite as much. You can use that time to survey the damage done. Which buttons have the most footprints on them? Which ones are only receiving peripheral damage? That is to say, *where do your priorities lie?*

You can identify the button that is taking the most damage by answering the question, *Where am I feeling as though I have to do something, rather than as though I get to do something?*

Where you are feeling entirely other-driven is most likely the button that is in most need of resetting. Now you can focus on that button; resetting it will more than likely help to reset the buttons receiving peripheral stamping. So how do you shift your focus? How can you turn this problem into an opportunity? Where is the truth that you can use to combat your deceptive Saboteur?

In many cases both in life and in dealing with your own personal Noid, it may be best to simply walk away from the argument. One of the Saboteur's tactics is to take a tactical defeat by forcing you into what's called a Pyrrhic victory. A Pyrrhic victory – named for Greek ruler Pyrrhus, who pioneered the technique – is one in which the cost of winning is ultimately greater for the victor than for the vanquished. Pyrrhus threw so many of his own troops at the Romans in two success-ful military campaigns against them that when news of the second victory reached him he was heard to reply, "Another such victory over the Romans and we are undone."

The Saboteur does not necessarily need to claim victory in his argument with you in order to achieve his goal. One tactic he employs is to so entangle you in the argument that your time, your energy or both are so depleted as to prevent you from achieving your goal once you win it. By the time you are finished formu-lating your logical explanations and counterarguments, the day is over or you are so mentally exhausted that actually completing the task which the Saboteur was trying to convince you against is impossible. In the end, it is fruitless to continue the argument.

Ask yourself, "Why am I trying to reason with the unreasonable?" Ultimately, in some cases you must simply break off negotiations with yourself and simply do the task that you need to do or say what you need to say, lest you claim victory in battle but lose the war. Leave open to yourself the option to just walk away from the argument. In fact, a better solution is not to engage in the argument at all – instead of arguing, get on with the doing and the being!

As I've said before, it is incredibly important to accept that buttons are going to be pushed. When you go through life expecting – or demanding – that no one and nothing will push your buttons, the frustration that occurs when those buttons inevitably get pushed can trigger emotional reactions, physical reactions and ultimately behavior that is at the best undesirable and at the worst destructive.

> Part of the power that positive thinking has lies in turning a problem into an opportunity; seeing a conflict as an opportunity for improvement.

Just as there's no shortage to the benefits that can come from expecting good things to happen, the pitfalls that will result from refusing to expect bad things to happen are bottomless. Part of the power that positive thinking has lies in turning a problem into an opportunity; seeing a conflict as an opportunity for improvement. Demanding a problem-free life means walking right into those pitfalls and having no way of getting out.

When you expect buttons to be pushed, the logical upside presents itself almost immediately. If buttons are going to be pushed, that must mean that every button can be reset. And if every button can be reset, then having one pushed must not be such a bad thing, after all! Button-pushing is not the end of the world, and part of resetting is realizing that fact. Life can, in fact, go back to the way it was before the button got pushed, and you can go back to living by your core values.

The battle with the Saboteur is, in the end, a battle between your Natural and your Adaptive selves. The Natural self does what feels right, what it wants. The Adaptive self does what is most appropriate for the situation it is in, and many times what it feels it *is called to* do.

> The Saboteur is the representation of your own fear of success and the responsibilities that success demands.

Knowing what we know about the Saboteur, we can surmise that the Saboteur can represent either one of these selves, depending upon which one suits its purpose. The Saboteur is neither Natural nor Adaptive; simply put, The Saboteur is the representation of your own fear of success and the responsibilities that success demands. He, or she, or *it*, is the ultimate self-limiter, exploiting fear and apprehension to define for you both how and who you are. *It* wants to squelch the natural, vibrant 'you' within you, making you into a creature of fear and limitation like itself. *It* wants you to feel as if you are enduring life rather than experiencing it, that you must hold your breath and duck whether the object flying at you is a brick or a feather.

You have to be able to breathe out, stand up, and face what's coming at you, which means facing down The Saboteur.

The 'E' for this chapter stands for *Emphasize core values*, but it could also very well stand for *Exhale*. In the 'R' chapter we talked about the initial physical reactions that occur when a button is pushed, physical reactions that take place before we even know that a button has been pushed.

One of those reflexes is that we inhale. We take a deep breath, storing oxygen as part of our involuntary fight-or-flight response. Our bodies know that a stressor is near, and our natural instinct is to make the choice between physically defending ourselves and running for cover, both of which require oxygen.

The techniques I've laid out in this chapter are ways in which you can exhale. By realizing that *fight* and *flight* are not your only two options – in fact, when in a confrontation with your Saboteur, they are not real options at all – you also realize that neither the defenses you've put up, nor the protective and combative mind-set that you are in, nor the extra oxygen you've inhaled are necessary. You can let all of those things go, and you can think clearly. You can exhale and enjoy.

CHAPTER FIVE: TAKE STOCK

CHAPTER FIVE: TAKE STOCK

> Basic animal nature mandates that we see any change
> in our lifestyle or environment as a
> Problem.

Of course, the ultimate goal of this method is to help you to move forward, shifting in your overall way of thinking. In the end, you need to be able to go from using these tactics in response to specific stimuli to turning them into a general attitude. You need to be able to make them part of your lifestyle, so that the RE-SET steps are used in response to all stimuli, whether you see a stimulus as positive or negative. Ultimately, the way that we as people make that transition has to do with the way in which we allow ourselves to perceive stimuli.

The first step in your perception shift must occur in that "positive vs. negative" realm. Basic animal nature mandates that we see any change in our lifestyle or environment as a Problem. Fight-or-flight instincts immediately label that Problem as a Threat, and our defenses go up accordingly. We either block out the change completely, work as hard as we possibly can to ignore it, or expend extra energy coexisting beside it without interacting. This is a *maintenance cycle*. In the case of button-pushing stimuli, what we are maintaining here is our own Ego.

Stop, Mary Elizabeth! The last thing I need is psychobabble, much less hundred-plus-year-old psychobabble! That's true. But when I speak about Ego, what I'm really talking about is the exact same thing I've been talking about throughout this book: the way we see the world around us, which ultimately is a reflection of the way we see ourselves. Ego is, quite simply, the way we believe things are, the way we believe circumstances should go and the way we believe people should act. In a maintenance cycle, all energy and effort is geared towards keeping these beliefs intact, towards *maintaining* our view of the world.

Please keep in mind that this is a natural human reaction. In fact, it's a natural reaction, period. During a lightning storm, a hamster can become so traumatized that it suffers a heart attack and dies. Stop talking to a pet parrot and it will become depressed and withdrawn, shedding feathers and refusing to eat. Take a whale from the sea and place it in captivity and it will refuse to mate. These are all reactions to what is perceived as a negative change in environment, external stimulus, or belief in the way the world works. So there's no need to think that your natural human behavior is in any way an overreaction. At least you're not a hamster in a storm!

The problem with this behavior is that change is inevitable. We no longer live in a time when a person can hole up in a cave somewhere and shut the rest of the world out. I'm pretty sure that, even in the deepest darkest cave, there's probably a WiFi hotspot.

Change is not going to possibly occur at some time in the future. Change *will* occur, and it is occurring all of the time. In order to adapt to the world around us, and in order to work with others in our workplace and industry, we must be able to react in an unnatural way towards change. We must cease seeing each Problem as a Threat, and instead, see it as an Opportunity.

> Opportunity means possibility …

Think about this example. Annie has a history of being disagreeable. She's a contrarian by nature, a co-worker you dread being paired up with on a project. She loves to stir up trouble amongst her fellow employees and has a tendency to be very emotional and explosive. Even on the simplest assignment, she refuses to carry out any task strictly according to instructions, opting to go against the grain to accomplish the goal.

Suddenly, Annie is working the way you want her to work. She's getting along with her co-workers, listening to others' ideas, and complaining much less. When she does speak against an assignment or a way of doing things, it is in a constructive way, with a logical argument behind the dissent. She hasn't blown up at you or at anyone else in two solid weeks.

This is a positive change in your workplace, am I right? However, it still challenges your worldview. It challenges the way you think that Annie should act, not in terms of how one should act in your workplace, but in terms of how Annie should act as herself. You're not alone in your unease, either; all of your co-workers are uncomfortable with the new Annie, because they still hold an old view of her.

"She's acting properly now, but what happens when she loses her cool?"

"Does she mean these things she's saying, or is she just saying what we want to hear?"

"Why is she doing this? Is she afraid of losing her job? Is she trying for a promotion I don't know about? What gives?"

The simple fact is that neither you nor your co-workers trust that Annie has changed for the right reasons, and so you see her change as a Problem, as a Threat. Your defenses go up and, rather than enjoying the benefits of Annie's current behavior, you simply wait for the other shoe to drop. You are unable to take advantage of her productivity, and in fact work in counter to it, creating more of a gridlock than existed previous to her change. You are stuck in a maintenance cycle, your mistrust runs rampant and you slow production and office chemistry to a crawl. But when you are able to move into a Growth Cycle, you can help cultivate what Annie is bringing to the table.

A Growth Cycle occurs when you cease seeing Changes and Problems as Threats, and instead see them as *Opportunities*. Opportunity means possibility, which opens doors. Threat only closes doors, out of a real or perceived need for protection.

Remember what we said about The Saboteur trying to "protect" you from success? Success could come from this situation with Annie, if you think about it. If you see her new behavior as an Opportunity, then it doesn't really matter whether she's "faking" her helpfulness, drive and willingness to cooperate or not. The reaction you give her can act as a sort of reward for her new behavior. This way, even in the worst-case scenario that she has modified her behavior only on a superficial level either to avoid termination or to secure promotion, Annie will see that her new demeanor is getting better results than the Mary Mary Quite Contrary she was before. And that works out for everybody.

When your behavior becomes constructive in this way, it is a manufactured reaction. I won't pretend for a second that humans naturally live in a Growth Cycle. We don't. But the ability to see change as Opportunity rather than as a Threat is a manufactured reaction which can *become* natural.

When practiced enough, any reaction becomes second nature. Your emotional muscle memory soon gets used to reacting with a positive and constructive perception rather than with fight-or-flight instinct, and the Growth Cycle becomes instinct.

Take a look at the contrast between the two cycles below:

Change Cycles

Growth Cycle

Maintenance Cycle

As you can see by the splitting arrows coming from the "Change/Problem" bubble at center, there is a very fine line – the width of a moment's hesitation – between moving into a Growth Cycle and a Maintenance Cycle. The difference is one between merely surviving and truly thriving.

Would you rather your Ego, your way of life and perception of the world and of yourself, merely tread water and survive? Or would you rather it thrive, growing and changing and adapting to the world around it, while using the situations the world throws its way to grow stronger and more successful?

These are not rhetorical questions, and the answers vary from person to person. But ask them of yourself: *Do I want to thrive, or am I content surviving?*

This book is for the Thrivers. This book is for the Survivors who want to be Thrivers.

And if you truly want to move beyond survival and begin to really see change and positive results in your work and in your life, you must take stock of yourself and of your attitude towards the world in general. Then take stock of the actions you have taken in order to get where you want to be. Think in these terms:

➤ *What do I feel?*

What emotions, thoughts, and physical reactions crop up on an everyday basis? We discussed a lot of this in our 'R' chapter: you need to continue to practice recognition throughout your day.

➤ *What do I want?*

What are your goals? Think about the short term as well as the long term. How do your daily actions move you closer to those goals? What is your overall goal, and how do your short- and long-term goals move you closer to it? Believe it or not, every action you take moves you in some direction relative to those goals. It is up to you to ensure that that direction is towards your desired destination rather than away from it.

➤ *What am I doing in order to get what I want?*

Again, consider your actions. Are they truly independent actions on your part, or are you merely reacting to those around you? Are you operating from your core values or being driven by the voice of your Saboteur?

➤ *Am I building new castles or simply protecting the one I already have?*

Here's what I mean: are your actions *defensive* or are they *constructive*? That is, do you do things in order to protect yourself and your worldview? Or do you attempt to create, to build new relationships, to move past old differences and past conflicts? Make a list of both defensive and constructive actions you've taken recently, and in relation to what perceived Threat or Opportunity you've taken them.

Once you've taken stock in this way, begin to move forward. Consult your list of defensive and constructive actions. For each defensive action, think of a positive constructive action you can take in the future to counteract the backwards motion you took. If that is not possible, list out possible constructive actions that you can take in the future should a similar situation arise.

> Ask yourself: Do I want to thrive, or am I content surviving?

When you are able to move in a positive direction rather than simply standing still and guarding what is already around you, you will have taken a significant step towards fully RESETting yourself. You'll be able to work towards disarming your buttons, rendering them impotent and obsolete.

CHAPTER SIX: DISARM

Chapter Six: DISARM

> We disarm, in effect, not by refusing to react to a button being pushed, but by giving other people no opportunity to push our buttons.

We have talked an awful lot in this book about resetting buttons that get pushed in the workplace, by family members and spouses, and out and about in the world in general. In the end, however, what you must do with these buttons is to learn how to disarm them; that is, you have to make it so that when circumstances which once pushed those buttons occur, they don't trigger the same behavioral reactions of your past. In the end, that's the only real way to prevent the chain reactions that can come from even the slightest tap of a button.

So how do we disarm? Do we accept that bad or frustrating things will occur in life, and try to look at them as insignificant in comparison to the vast scope of life? Do we simply go through life in a peaceful state, allowing all distractions and annoyances to roll off of us like water off a duck's back? Do we tame our own personalities, going along with what others require of us so as to avoid any conflict?

No. Of course not. All three of these solutions are simplistic and, in the end, detrimental to our mental, emotional and ultimately to our physical health. Yes, annoying, frustrating and even combative situations will take place in our lives. And yes, we will react to those things. Believe it or not, it's okay and even healthy to blow up every once in a while. If you keep everything bottled up inside instead of occasionally letting some of it escape, you're gift-wrapping a heart attack for yourself later in life.

We disarm, in effect, not by refusing to react to a button being pushed, but by giving other people no opportunity to push our buttons. We are able to rob others of this opportunity by living a self-directed life-style, making our own choices and decisions rather than allowing others to direct us. Too often in life we accord ourselves victim status, insisting that other people have more control over our lives than we do.

"I have to work overtime or my boss will kill me!"

"I'd better get the living room picked up or my wife will have a fit!"

"I had to skip my break today because Chris spilled food on the floor and I had to help him clean it up."

"What am I going to do? I have no choice but to…" (the Invisible Authority)

Do these sound familiar? No matter which stage of life we're at, all of us at one point or another have accorded inconvenient or uncomfortable circumstances to someone else, someone or something we perceive to have power or control over our lives. The fact is that there's no reason you *have* to work overtime, no reason you *have* to pick up the living room, and no reason you *have* to help Chris pick up that mess. To do these things is a choice that you yourself make. It is in realizing that you have made this choice, or that you have made the opposite choice, that self-directed, responsible living begins.

Personal Responsibility

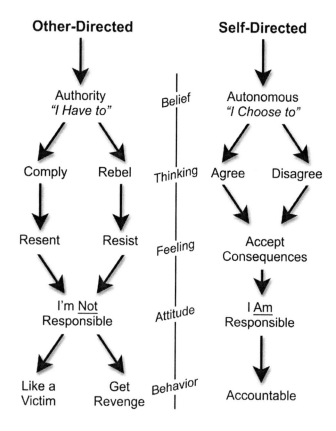

A Self-Directed Person knows that each activity in
which a person can participate is the result
of a choice...

In this graphic you can see the differences between self-directed living and other-directed living. It is a model that the Integro Leadership Institute uses to illustrate the ideal way of looking at the forces that surround us, and I think that it is an important key in learning how to disarm our buttons.

Let us for a moment take a look at this model in depth and determine those behaviors and actions in which we can engage that will help us to live a more self-directed life.

First, let's look at the left-hand column. When we believe that we are subject to authority, we are living an other-directed life. Because the Authority Figure says, "Do it," the Other-Directed Person says "I have to do it." There are then only two options: either comply with Authority, or rebel against Authority. Complying with an Authority Figure's decree rather than doing what we'd like to do creates resentment, along with a helplessness. Rebelling against an Authority Figure means that you must expend a good deal of energy to resist that decree. There may be negative consequences for your rebellion.

Pay attention to the flow chart here! Notice that no matter which choice you make, in the end it all leads to the same place: "I'm *not* responsible!" Perceiving oneself as having no responsibility in one's own life also results in feeling powerless over one's own life. In the end, the Other-Directed Person may feel victimized, may feel as if he or she deserves revenge against Authority, or – worst of all– feels and behaves like a vengeful victim.

By way of comparison, take a look at the Self-Directed Person's column. A self-directed person is not subject to authority in his or her own mind, but rather makes autonomous choices in every avenue of life. Even when accidents or unforeseen events occur, Self-Directed People understand that they have made the choice to put themselves in the situations in which those events can take place. The clause "I choose to…" replaces "I have to…" at the beginning of every sentence.

In other words, the recognition of choice is the defining characteristic of a Self-Directed Person. A Self-Directed Person knows that each activity in which a person can participate is the result of a choice, not an obligation foisted upon him or her by some authority figure. A person who realizes that choice exists looks at a task or assignment and chooses to agree with that assignment and carry it out or to disagree with it and opt to do something else instead. Compare this to the Other-Directed Person, who while still making essentially the same choice – *do I perform the task or not?* – makes it with an entirely different perception.

The difference between the Other-Directed and Self-Directed person rests primarily in the next spot on our flow chart. Whereas on the left side we saw Other-Directed people resent or resist both their duties and the person they saw as an Authority Figure, Self-Directed people are defined by their ability to accept the consequences of whatever action they take. Rather than pushing responsibility for their actions on some other reason – *"I had to do it,"* or *"She made me say that"* – Self-Directed people know that they have made the choice to do one thing or the other; in some instances, they have made the choice not to make a choice. Knowing that option exists is also part of being Self-Directed.

In the end, disarming one's buttons means taking away the power of others to push those buttons. The buttons, of course, still exist. If pushed, they will most likely elicit similar reactions to those they provoked before. However, the Self-Directed person, the truly *Disarmed* person, has taken that ability away from anyone who might do any pushing, simply by remembering that there is always a choice!

Once you've disarmed, you'll truly be the only person who can push your buttons. It doesn't happen right away, and it isn't by any means easy. If you are willing to work, and if you are willing to take responsibility for your choices, actions and inactions, you will empower yourself to first RESET, and then to DISARM your buttons.

AFTERWORD

AFTERWORD

At the beginning of this book, I said that the inspiration for the "RESET Your Buttons" concept was my mother, who told me that I let other people push my buttons too much and too often. It is fitting, then, to end this book by telling you that, during the writing of the book, my mother suffered a massive heart attack and, after a week in hospice, passed away in December of 2007. On my brother's birthday, about an hour after she sang "Happy Birthday" to him over the phone, she began having symptoms of cardiac arrest and was rushed to the hospital. In just a few hours, my family and I had to make the difficult decision to honor her wishes and remove her from life support, forgo any further surgery and move her into hospice. During the months that followed, my life was turned upside down as I dealt with the aftershocks, the impending grief and accepting the decisions my family and I chose to make on her behalf.

This is to say nothing of what such a major life event did to my personal schedule. The book had to be put on hold, my consulting firm -- S.T.A.R. Resources -- had to be put on hold, and my personal life along with holiday planning also had to be put on hold. These seem like petty and selfish things when held up against something so massive as the incapacitation and death of a parent, but they are issues and buttons pressed none-theless. As much as we need and want to rise above personal obligations and selfish desires when a family member is in need, their need and its pull upon us can be an inconvenience. It conflicts with our expectations and our plans. It, in other words, pushes buttons.

In this case, it was as if someone had picked up my switchboard and dropped it, face-first, onto the floor. Every button that could possibly be pushed was pushed, and at the same time. I had to figure out how to RESET: how to meet my obligations to my mother, my family, my clients and to myself, and how to do it without re-sentment, instead remembering the power of choice. I had to choose from an open, yet saddened, heart filled with love, understanding, empathy and compassion. These are issues that all of us have to deal with at various points in our lives, and in order to do so productively and in peace we have to learn how to RESET.

This morning, when I got up to write this afterword, some entity threw a handful of rocks at my switchboard, hitting buttons at random. My husband was gone, having gone out to gas up our car only to find that there wasn't any gas anywhere. The gas stations in Charlotte, N.C. had run dry. I had a scheduled conference call that I missed because my phone was unplugged, and I had lost several voicemails. I had to call clients and partners back, but before I could do that I had to RESET.

Sanity, at its core, is about taking a step back to breathe and realizing that, in life, nothing is promised. Nothing is predictable. For the sake of yourself and your own sanity, choose to engage coping skills. Use the RESET Mindset.

Wishing the problem away doesn't work, and neither does venting until you feel better. Hopeful though you feel, vented though you are, the problem is that the problem is still there. Instead of reacting, rebelling, and resisting, simply remember (the steps to) RESETTING!

So first, Recognize. Recognize that life happens, and that you need to regain a sense of normalcy. Recognize the stress and physical reactions that your body has to a button being pushed, whether it's a phone call telling you that a loved one has passed or it's a phone call missed when the phone is unplugged. Recognition of the physical things that are happening to you is key to working through the problem causing that stress.

The reason that you have these reactions is that your expectations for the day, for the week, for the circumstances surrounding your life have been challenged or shattered. Something that you expected to happen is either not happening or is occurring differently.

Do you need to RESET your expectations? **Keep in mind that expectations are necessary, but that they are self-promises, not universal guarantees.**

Have a good sense of yourself. Who are you? Do whatever it takes to know yourself better. To know oneself is, in fact, the ultimate journey. Know yourself better than anyone else can know you; know the good, the bad, the dark and the light about yourself. Know who and what runs you. Who and what do you *allow* to run you? Clarify your own limitations to yourself, and then identify which limitations are acceptable and which ones you want to eliminate or diminish. What are you willing to accept about yourself, and what about yourself are you happy to accept?

Remember, at the end of the day, there truly is no such thing as being out of control. Either you control yourself or you choose to allow some other set of circumstances to control you. The question is which you allow to have power over you – yourself or your surroundings?

Know your core values. The best way to identify these values is to ask yourself, *What are my beliefs? What am I willing to stand for? What am I willing to fight for?* Your core values are those beliefs for which the fight is always worth it, no matter the immediate circumstances.

Stress, addiction, depression and failure are all rooted in being in resistance to *what is.* We want our circumstances to be different than what they are, but we fight against what is without accepting that what is, *is.* We *must* accept that fact, then choose to do something about that which we can control.

In many cases, resistance to the status quo is futile – when my mother was in hospice, it was useless to fight against the reality that she was going to leave us. The facts must be accepted. Accept the status quo as reality even as you fight against it – a dissatisfying work situation, for example, *is* a dissatisfying work situation; accept that fact before you can work to change it.

Within these circumstances, your core values will carry you through. When my mother had her heart attack, it would have done no good to pretend that she was not going to die. The situation was unalterable. My core values – those of family, of honoring my mother's wishes regarding her last months and moments on Earth, of caring for my siblings, they for me and us for our families throughout that period of time – carried me through a situation I did not want to experience and from which I could not escape.

Remember: the further away from your core values you move, the more excuses you will make for compromising them. Continually remind yourself of your values; failure to do so is a slippery slope towards losing them completely.

What are the actions that you have to take in order to reinforce your core values? Take stock of what you're already doing to operate within those values. Take stock of the people and factors in your life that are supporting those core values. Take stock of how often your buttons get pushed. Take stock of your use of the RESET process. How often are you able to reset? How much do you need to RESET before you disarm?

Life being the spiral that it is, the goal and idea is that the more you understand where these buttons are, the less and less often a particular button can be pushed in a particular way. Eventually it can't be pushed at all.

Remember also that, as the game gets bigger, the tests you undergo get tougher and tougher. Little things don't push buttons as easily; it takes something much larger.

I'll leave you with one final piece of advice. When you stake a claim to living your life a certain way, you will be immediately barraged with external factors and stimuli which test that claim. In another manner of speaking, you will be barraged with opportunities to make that change, to strengthen your new muscle!

Be ready, prepared, even excited to test your claim. Live the life you want to live in the face of your buttons being pushed; in the end, you'll be able to celebrate every time you RESET.

Celebrate disarming your buttons once and for all. I came through the loss of my mother celebrating, because I came through it intact. I was strong enough, my core values were strong enough, my ability to RESET was strong enough to carry me through it. Because I had used the very steps I've taught you in these pages, I was able to relate to friends, family and clients in a loving, productive and constructive way. I continued to be a functioning woman, while saying goodbye to my mom. My family stayed intact and healthy, even without its matriarch.

By engaging these tools – by **R**ecognizing buttons being pushed, by understanding your **E**xpectations, by defining your **S**ense of self, by **E**mphasizing your core values, by Taking stock – you can come through some of life's most stressful and chaotic situations whole. You will be able to do it because you stood for what you know, and because you took that stand for those whom you love and care about. People will walk away saying, "I like and know myself better for having been with you."

More importantly, you will be able to say, "I like and know myself better." In the end, that's what this journey has been about, friends. Thank you for being a part of mine.

In the end, disarming one's buttons means
taking away the power of others to
push those buttons.